SLEEPING BEAUTY

EEPING
EAUTY

Based on Walt Disney Productions' full length cartoon feature film

This adaptation by
Guy N Smith

NEW ENGLISH LIBRARY
TIMES MIRROR

Other stories from Disney cartoon feature films and available in the NEL series

DUMBO

LADY AND THE TRAMP

SNOW WHITE AND THE SEVEN DWARFS

SONG OF THE SOUTH

ROBIN HOOD

PINOCCHIO

FIRST NEL PAPERBACK EDITION SEPTEMBER 1975

NEL Books are published by
New English Library Limited from Barnard's Inn,
Holborn, London EC1.
Made and printed in Great Britain by
Hunt Barnard Printing Ltd, Aylesbury, Bucks.
Typesetting by The Yale Press Ltd, London SE25

45002692 2

SLEEPING BEAUTY

CHAPTER ONE

Once upon a time in a faraway land there lived a king and his fair queen. For many years they had longed for a child, and then, when they had almost given up hope, their wish was granted. A baby daughter was born to them, and they named her Aurora after the dawn, for she had filled their lives with sunshine.

People travelled from far and wide to see her. One day the king proclaimed a special holiday throughout the kingdom so that everybody, poor and rich alike, might come and pay homage to the infant princess.

The sun shone brightly and the streets were crowded with people waving banners, shouting and singing:

On that joyful day! On that joyful day!
Joyfully now, to our Princess we come,
Bringing gifts and all good wishes too.
We pledge our loyalty anew,
Hail to the Princess Aurora!
All of her subjects adore her!
Hail to the King! Hail to the Queen!
Hail to the Princess Aurora!
Health to the Princess! Wealth to the Princess!
Long live the Princess Aurora!

Everybody was converging on the castle where the Princess lived, high upon the hill above the village. Knights in shining armour rode their horses across the narrow bridge, and everywhere birds were singing. The people were happier than they had ever been.

Inside the castle, King Stefan and his Queen were seated on their thrones in the long throne-room. They, too, were happy, for the whole kingdom was now celebrating the birth of their beautiful daughter.

A line of trumpeters clad in scarlet uniforms raised their trumpets and a herald began to read in a loud voice from a scroll of parchment.

'Their Royal Highnesses,' he announced, 'King Hubert and Prince Phillip!'

The king and his small son approached the throne. The two kings, their crowns glinting and their long robes trailing behind them, smiled and embraced. It was the dream of these monarchs that one day their kingdoms would be united, and so today they were to announce to the people thronging outside the castle that the dark-haired child, Prince Phillip, Hubert's son and heir, was to be betrothed to Stefan's daughter, Aurora.

Prince Phillip stood apart from the embracing monarchs, and looked down into the cradle where his future bride lay. Up above, three sparkling lights floated gently down a sunbeam which filtered in through one of the castle windows, and as they neared the ground they suddenly changed shape. Three tiny figures alighted, and the watching people gasped as they recognised them as fairies.

'Their most honoured and exalted excellencies,' the herald boomed. 'The Three Good Fairies — Mistress Flora, Mistress Fauna, and Mistress Merryweather!'

The Three Good Fairies their faces wreathed in smiles, flew past the line of subjects and trumpeters, and alighted on the side of the cradle.

'Ah! The little darling!' they sighed, and then they took off again, this time coming to rest in front of the King and Queen.

'Your Majesties,' they bowed, Flora speaking for all of them. 'Each of us the child may bless, with a single gift, no more, no less.'

With this Flora flew back to the cradle, while the people watched in awe. The fairy waved her wand, and before their very eyes

flowers began to shower down and settle in the cradle.

'Little Princess,' Flora chanted in a tiny musical voice, 'my gift shall be the gift of Beauty.'

Everybody began to sing:

One gift, Beauty rare,
Gold of sunshine in her hair,
Lips that shame the red red rose
She'll walk in springtime wherever she goes.

Fauna joined Flora at the cradle. At the wave of her wand, birds came gliding in,

chirping and twittering, and suddenly the onlookers saw a vision of a distant castle appear before their very eyes. At a window of the castle a girl was sitting, a bird perched on her finger. Then the scene faded, and sparkling lights drifted down to the cradle.

'Tiny Princess,' Fauna chanted, 'my gift shall be the gift of Song.'

Once more the watching people burst into song:

One gift, the gift of Song,
Melody her whole life long,
The Nightingale's her troubadour,
Bringing his sweet serenade to her door.

Merryweather advanced on the cradle, her wand held aloft.

'Sweet Princess,' she chanted, 'my gift shall be the . . .'

Her words were drowned in a rush of wind as the castle doors blew wide open. A veritable gale howled in, the banners on the walls flapping wildly and the elaborate dresses and gowns of the people being blown in all directions. The King and Queen clutched at their robes. The clear blue skies outside had become suddenly overcast. Thunder rumbled and lightning flashed.

'What is all this?' King Stefan shouted, but his words were lost to the wind.

The hall was growing darker by the second. The Three Good Fairies huddled together, alarmed expressions on their faces. As suddenly as it had begun, the wind dropped, and then they saw a wispy flame appear in the centre of the hall, flickering and gradually taking on a definite shape. It burned brighter and then changed into a human form. The face was that of a sharp-featured female with an evil sneer. She wore a pointed hat and long flowing black robes; in her hand she, too, carried a wand.

'Why, it's Maleficent!' Fauna cried in alarm. 'The wicked Witch! What does she want here?'

On Maleficent's shoulder perched a raven, its jet black plumage matching her own clothing. She advanced until she was standing before the two kings and the Three Good Fairies.

'Well,' she sneered. 'Quite a glittering assemblage, King Stefan. Royalty, nobility, the gentry, and oh, ha, ha, ha, how quaint... even the rabble!'

'Oh dear!' Merryweather whispered in alarm.

The Raven jumped from Maleficent's shoulder to her staff, croaking in agreement with its mistress. Maleficent glared at the King and Queen.

'I really felt quite distressed at not receiving an invitation,' she said, with a menacing tone in her voice.

'You weren't wanted, Maleficent!' It was Merryweather who spoke the thoughts of everybody present.

Maleficent artfully pretended to be embarrassed.

'Not wanted?' she muttered, turning to pet her raven. 'Not wanted? Oh dear, what an awkward situation! I hoped that it was merely due to some oversight. Well, in that event, I'd best be on my way!'

A sigh of relief was uttered by everybody present, for secretly they all feared Maleficent.

'And you're not offended, your excellency?'

The Queen hoped that the matter would be resolved peacefully.

Maleficent regarded the Queen for some moments before replying.

'Why no, Your Majesty,' she smiled, with a wickedness that the enshrouding darkness concealed. 'And to show that I bear no ill will, I, too, shall bestow a gift on the child. Listen well, all of you!'

The Raven flew back on to her shoulder and she banged on the ground with her staff.

'The Princess shall indeed grow in grace and beauty,' she cried, 'beloved by all who know her.'

Once more the assembled people witnessed a vision. In the midst of the darkness a spinning-wheel and a girl appeared, while bats fluttered menacingly in the air.

'But before the sun sets on her sixteenth birthday,' Maleficent went on in a high-pitched voice, 'she shall prick her finger on the spindle of a spinning-wheel and die!'

With a sob of anguish the Queen darted to the cradle and clasped the baby to her.

'Oh, no!' she wept. 'Please, *no!*'

'Seize that creature!' cried Stefan, pointing to Maleficent.

At the King's command three armed guards leapt forward to do his bidding. Just as their hands reached out for the Witch, she became screened in a protective wall of flames. They stood transfixed.

'Stand back, you fools!' she snarled.

As the guards fell back, Maleficent disappeared in a cloud of fire and smoke. Only her raven remained, and with a flapping of jet black wings he, too, flew off through the open doors.

CHAPTER TWO

For a few moments there was silence except for the weeping of the Queen. King Stefan slipped a comforting arm around her.

'Don't despair, Your Majesties,' Flora implored them. 'Merryweather still has her gift to give.'

Stefan turned to the Three Good Fairies.

'Then . . . she can undo this fearful curse?' he asked.

'Oh, no sire,' Flora replied. 'Maleficent's powers are far too great!'

A look of despair appeared on the King's face.

'But she can help,' Fauna consoled him.

Merryweather waved her wand. The dark clouds summoned by the Wicked Fairy began to disappear and the sky lightened as the sun broke through. A girl on a bier floated downwards, turned into a ray of magic, and descended to the floor.

'But . . .' Merryweather hesitated.

'Just do your best, dear,' Fauna encouraged.

'Yes, go on,' Flora pleaded.

Meryweather drew herself up, and holding her wand skywards, she started to speak:

Sweet Princess,
If through this wicked Witch's trick,
A spindle should your finger prick,
A ray of hope there still may be,
In this the Gift I give to thee
Not in death, but just sleep,
The fateful prophecy you'll keep,
And from this slumber you shall wake,
When true love's kiss the spell shall break.

'For true love conquers all,' chorused the people.

However, King Stefan was still fearful for his daughter's life. Immediately he decreed that every spinning-wheel in the kingdom should be burned on that very day. His wishes were carried out. Everyone who possessed a spinning-wheel fetched it, and a massive bonfire was made of them in the courtyard, the flames licking hungrily at the huge pile.

The Three Good Fairies stood watching this from the window of the throne-room.

'Oh, silly fiddle-faddle!' Flora tried to convince everyone, including herself, that there was no truth in the Witch's curse.

'Now, come on, let's have a nice cup of tea,' Fauna said. 'I'm sure it'll work out somehow.'

She waved her wand, and teacups and a teapot appeared. She began to pour the tea, and handed a cup to her two companions.

'Well, a bonfire won't stop Maleficent!' muttered Merryweather, sipping her tea gloomily.

'Of course not,' Flora agreed. 'But what will?'

'Well, perhaps if we reason with her . . .' Fauna suggested.

'Reason?' Flora gasped. 'With Maleficent?'

'Well, she can't be all that bad,' Fauna argued, but she did not sound very convincing.

'Oh yes she can!' Flora snapped.

'I'd like to turn her into a flat old hoptoad!' cried Merryweather, bouncing up and down with rage.

'Now dear, that isn't a very nice thing to say.' Fauna never liked to think bad things of anybody.

'Besides, we can't,' Fauna added. 'You know our magic doesn't work that way. It can only do good, dear: to bring joy and happiness.'

'Well, that would make me very happy!' Merryweather stamped her foot.

'But there must be some way,' Flora mused. After a few moments of deep thought she snapped, 'There is!'

'There is?' Merryweather gasped.

'Whatever is it, Flora?' Fauna asked eagerly.

'I'm going to . . . shhh!' Flora suddenly checked herself. 'Even walls have ears. Follow me!'

Flora and Fauna made themselves very small, and flying past Merryweather they dropped into an open box which stood nearby. Shaking her head in amazement, Merryweather also made herself small, and followed them. Between them they pulled the lid down. The interior of the box was empty except for a small silver spoon.

'I'll turn her into a flower,' Flora whispered.

'Maleficent?' Merryweather asked in surprise.

'No, no dear, the Princess,' Flora replied.

'She'd make a lovely flower. Don't you see, a flower can't prick its finger. It hasn't got any fingers. She'll be perfectly safe like that!'

'Until Maleficent sends a frost!' Merryweather replied impatiently.

'Oh, dear! I never thought of that!' Flora looked crestfallen.

'She always ruins your nicest flowers,' Fauna reminded her.

The Three Good Fairies sat down deep in thought.

'You're right,' Flora moaned. 'And she'll be expecting us to do something like that.'

'Oh, well,' Merryweather looked crestfallen. 'What won't she be expecting? She knows everything.'

'That's just where you're wrong, dear,' Fauna smiled. 'Maleficent doesn't know anything about love, or kindness, or the joy of helping others. You know, sometimes I don't think she's really very happy.'

'That's it!' Flora began to cheer up. 'Of course, it's the only thing she can't understand, and won't expect either! Now, we'll have to plan it carefully. Let's see. The woodcutter's cottage. Yes, yes, the abandoned one. Of course, the King and Queen will object, but when we explain that it's the only way . . .'

'Explain what?' Merryweather was puzzled, and her pretty little face wrinkled up into a frown.

'About the three peasant women raising a foundling child deep in the forest.'

'Oh,' and even Fauna was at a loss to understand what Flora was talking about. 'Well, that's very nice of them. Who are they?'

Flora stood up, smiled mysteriously, and

waved her wand. In a flash the Three Good Fairies were transformed into three peasant women, their clothes torn and ragged. In amazement Merryweather and Fauna gazed at their reflections in one of the teacups.

'Why . . . uh . . .' Merryweather gasped. 'It's *us*! You mean we . . .?'

'Yes,' Flora smiled. 'We must take care of the baby.'

'Oh, I'd like that.' Fauna said.

'Well, yes, so would I,' Merryweather added. 'We'd have to feed it, and wash it, and rock it, and . . . oh, I'd love it! You really think we can?'

'If humans can do it, so can we!' Flora stated.

'And we'd have your magic to help us,' Merryweather went on.

'No!' Flora shook her head. *'No magic!'*

With that Flora moved close to the other two, and took Fauna's wand and wings from her. Merryweather backed away, a look of horror on her face.

'I'll take those wands right now!' Flora cried, 'and you'd better get rid of those wings as well!'

'You mean live like mortals?' Merryweather gasped. 'For sixteen years?'

With that Merryweather fluttered up into the air, in an attempt to escape. Suddenly, Flora waved her wand. Merryweather's wings disappeared and she fell back, landing in the spoon.

'But . . . but,' Merryweather gasped, picking herself up and hiding behind Fauna, 'we . . . we don't know how . . . we've never done anything without magic!'

'And that's why Maleficent will never suspect,' said Flora, a cunning gleam in her eye.

'But . . . but who'll wash and cook?' Merryweather asked.

'We'll all take turns, help each other,' Flora answered.

'I'll take care of the baby,' Fauna said eagerly.

'Come along now,' said Flora, opening the box and hopping out. 'We must tell Their Majesties at once.'

King Stefan listened as the Three Good Fairies stood before himself and the Queen and told them of their plans. He knew that it was the only solution if Aurora was to live past her sixteenth birthday.

The Queen rose and, with tears in her eyes, lifted the baby princess from the cradle and passed her over to Flora.

The King and Queen watched with heavy hearts as their most precious possession, their only child, disappeared into the night.

Now they could only hope and pray.

CHAPTER THREE

Many sad and lonely years passed by for King Stefan and his people. However, as the time for the Princess's sixteenth birthday drew near the entire kingdom began to rejoice, for everybody knew that as long as Maleficent's domain, the Forbidden Mountains, thundered with her wrath and frustration, her evil prophecy had not yet been fulfilled.

In her mountain stronghold Maleficent paced up and down the long courtroom where her Goon warriors, the evil henchmen who carried out her bidding, stood in fear and trembling at the sight of her wrath.

'It's incredible!' she raged, her face contorted with anger. 'Sixteen years, and not a trace of her. She couldn't have vanished into thin air!'

The Goon leaders blinked, and shifted nervously from one foot to another.

'Are you sure you searched everywhere?' she snarled.

'Uh . . . uh . . . yep . . . yep . . . everywhere,' the chief Goon nodded. 'We all did.'

'And what about the town?' Maleficent thundered. 'The forests? The mountains?'

'Yeh,' the Goon leader tried to hide his fear. 'We searched the mountains, and . . . uh, uh . . . the houses . . . uh . . . uh . . . lemme see . . . uh, uh . . . and all the cradles.'

'Cradles!' shrieked the Witch, thrusting her evil face close to his.

'Uh, yep,' he recoiled in fear. 'Yep, every cradle.'

Maleficent turned to the raven which was perched on the arm of a nearby chair.

'Cradle!' she rasped. 'Did you hear that my pet? All these years they've been looking for a *baby*!'

She began to laugh hysterically.

'Fools! Idiots! Imbeciles!' With a sweep of her arm she conjured up thunder and lightning. With yells of terror the Goons began to run, bumping into each other, stumbling and falling into a heap at the bottom of a long flight of stone steps. Two of them picked themselves up, and continued to run.

With another snarl Maleficent hurled a thunderbolt, cutting off their retreat. Howls of anguish came from all the Goons as they began to squeeze themselves into cracks in the wall.

Maleficent walked back the length of the empty courtroom to her throne, followed by the raven. With a thoughtful expression on her face she seated herself, and the evil-looking bird, croaking softly, perched on her hand.

'You are my last hope,' she murmured gently, stroking the bird's head. 'Circle far and wide, search for a maid of sixteen with hair of sunshine gold and lips as red as the rose.'

With a final croak the raven fluttered up on to the battlements and looked back once before gliding off down the mountainside.

'Go, and do not fail me!' Maleficent's words followed him.

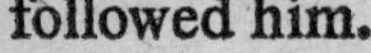

For sixteen long years the whereabouts of the Princess had remained a mystery. Deep in the forest, in a woodcutter's cottage, the Three Good Fairies had carried out their well-laid plan, and living like mortals they had reared the child as their own. They had renamed her Briar Rose.

In a clearing in the forest stood the neat little woodcutter's hut, ivy and honeysuckle growing round the door, and smoke wafting up from the chimney.

Briar Rose opened the window, and with a

smile of contentment on her face she shook out a duster. She was very happy for today was her sixteenth birthday, and the Good Fairies had planned a party for her, and also something extra special as a surprise.

The Good Fairies were grouped around a table poring over a book.

'Well, now how about this one?' Merryweather pointed to the page.

'This is the one I picked,' Flora remarked.

'She'll look beautiful in that,' Fauna added.

'Now, I thought just a few changes here,' Flora went on, holding up a picture of a dress. 'A pretty bow, and raise the shoulder line, and we'll need a few pleats.'

They dropped their voices to a whisper as Briar Rose came down the stairs dusting the rail.

'Yes, but how are we going to get her out of the house?' Merryweather voiced the problem that had been worrying them all.

'I'll think of something,' Flora promised.

'Well,' began Briar Rose, coming towards them, 'and what are you three dears up to?'

Hastily the Good Fairies closed the book.

'Up to?' Merryweather had a guilty expression on her face.

'Up to?' Flora had to think quickly. 'We . . . ah . . . we want you to go and pick some berries.'

'Berries!' Briar Rose looked surprised. 'But I picked some berries yesterday.'

'Oh . . . uh . . .' Flora muttered. 'We . . . we need more, dear. Lots more. Now you go off and pick them, and don't hurry back. There's plenty of time.'

'But don't go too far,' Merryweather added with a worried expression on her face. 'And don't speak to strangers.'

Briar Rose went and fetched a basket.

'Goodbye,' she called as she opened the door, and went outside.

'I wonder if she suspects,' Merryweather muttered as they watched Briar Rose going off into the forest.

'Of course not,' Flora laughed. 'Now come on, we've got a lot to do. Oh, will she be surprised!'

'Yes, and a dress that a Princess can be proud of,' Flora smiled, taking some material out of a wooden trunk. 'This material will make up into a beautiful dress.'

'I'll get the wands,' Merryweather made a move towards the staircase.

'Get the wands!' Flora echoed. 'Oh no! Remember what we said. No magic under any circumstances!'

'But the sixteen years are almost up,' Merryweather replied.

'We're taking no chances,' Flora had a determined expression on her face. 'Only a few more hours now.'

Fauna was already taking pots and pans out of a cupboard in the corner of the room.

'I'm going to bake the cake,' she announced proudly.

'You!' Merryweather began to laugh.

'She's always wanted to bake a cake,' Flora explained, 'and this is her last chance to do so without the help of magic.'

'Yes,' added Fauna, busying herself by wiping the table, 'I'm going to make it fifteen layers, and decorate it with pink and blue forget-me-knots.'

'And I'm going to make the dress,' Flora began laying the material out.

'But *you* can't sew, and *she's* never cooked!' Merryweather stood and looked at her two companions with her hands on her hips.

'All you do is follow the book,' said Flora, tossing the material into the air so that it fell over Merryweather's head, 'and you, my dear, can be the dummy.'

Soon they were all busy. Fauna stood at the table, the book propped up in front of her, measuring out cupfuls of flour. Flora produced a pair of scissors, and began to cut the material carefully.

'I still say we ought to use magic,' Merryweather's muffled voice came from beneath the cloth.

Soon there was a hole large enough for Merryweather's head to poke through.

'Oh, what a lovely shade,' Flora murmured.

'But I wanted it blue, not pink,' wailed Merryweather, whose enthusiasm was already failing. She was becoming cross at having to stand still for so long.

'Now, dear, we decided *pink* was her colour,' Flora murmured, snipping away.

'*You* decided!' Merryweather retorted, and then lapsed into silence.

'Two eggs, fold in gently. Fold? Oh, oh well.' Fauna had been paying too much attention to what the other two were doing.

'I can't breathe.' Merryweather was certainly bad-tempered. 'Let me out of here. It looks awful!'

2

'That's because it's on you, dear,' Flora replied good-naturedly.

'Oh, gracious, how that child has grown,' Flora went on, determined to distract Merryweather's attention. 'It seems only yesterday since we brought her here. She was just a tiny baby then. Now, she's a beautiful girl.'

As Flora busily pinned up the sleeves, tears began to roll down Merryweather's cheek.

'Why, Merryweather,' began Fauna, putting down her pots and pans. 'Whatever is the matter with you?'

'After today,' Merryweather sobbed, dabbing at her eyes with some of the cloth, 'she'll be a princess and safe from Maleficent, and then we won't have her any more.'

'Now, now,' Flora consoled her, deliberately turning her face away from the other two, 'we all knew this day had to come.'

'But why did it have to come so soon?' Fauna started to cry also.

'After all,' but Flora did not pause in her work, 'we've had her with us for sixteen years.'

'Sixteen wonderful years,' sniffed Merryweather.

'Oh, good gracious!' Flora turned to her two companions. 'We're acting like a lot of ninnies. C'mon she'll be back before we get started!'

CHAPTER FOUR

Out in the woods Briar Rose was enjoying herself picking berries. The sunlight filtered down through the overhanging branches, glistening on her long golden hair as she walked along the grassy path.

A bluebird, preening his feathers in a nearby tree, paused as he heard her footsteps. He peeped down. My, my! He never thought human beings could be so beautiful. Suddenly he fluttered down, and landed on a branch close to where Briar Rose would have to walk. There was another movement in the leaves close by. A cardinal poked its head out, and seeing that the bluebird had no fear of this lovely girl, he fluttered down to the same branch. As he did so the bluebird lost its footing, and fell down on to the carpet of leaves and grass beneath.

Briar Rose paused as she saw the fallen bluebird.

'Goodness me!' she exclaimed. 'You have taken a tumble, haven't you?'

With that she stooped, picked him up, and placed him back in the tree.

By now the woodland creatures were aware that the beautiful Briar Rose was in their

midst. Two rabbits popped up out of a fallen log; a squirrel which had been sleeping all morning suddenly woke up, and peered downwards. Likewise, an owl which would have slept until dusk, was awoken by the commotion around him, and as he emerged from his daytime roost to see what was going on, a scurrying squirrel bumped into him, and knocked him off the branch.

'Who! Who! Who!' hooted the owl as he fell into the basket carried by the passing Briar Rose.

Briar Rose smiled, and carried on walking, a host of woodland creatures following at her heels. At last they came to a log bridge which spanned a wide stream with mossy banks and waterlilies floating on it.

Some distance away amongst the trees, a handsome young man was riding a horse. When he heard Briar Rose singing, he hauled on the reins, causing his mount to rear and plunge.

'You hear that, Samson?' he asked, patting his horse's neck and listening intently. 'It's beautiful. What is it? Come on, let's find out. Aw, come on, for an extra bucket of oats and a few carrots? Hup, boy!'

The horse responded to the coaxing, and soon they were galloping through the trees, jumping over fallen logs with ease, the prince ducking his head to avoid low branches.

Suddenly, the Prince lost his hold on the reins, and before he knew what had happened he had fallen off and landed with a splash in a shallow stream. Shaken, but otherwise unhurt, he struggled to his feet, shaking the water from him.

'Hey! Whoa! Come back!' he yelled as the riderless horse went galloping on.

A hundred yards or so further on, the horse realised that its rider was no longer in the saddle. With a puzzled expression on its face it turned round, and began to retrace its steps. It saw the prince's hat lying on the ground, and clasping it firmly between its teeth, it went in search of its master.

The Prince was glad to see the return of his horse, fearing that he might have found himself wandering lost in the forest when night fell.

'No carrots!' He smacked the horse playfully with his hat, and gazed down at his sodden clothes.

Briar Rose paused beneath a large spreading tree, and accepted a flower which the owl held out to her with his beak. She continued to sing:

I wonder, I wonder,
I wonder why each little bird has a someone
to sing to,
Sweet things to,
A gay little love melody.
I wonder, I wonder,
If my heart keeps singing,
Will my song go winging,
To someone who'll find me and bring back
A love song to me.

As she sang more birds and a squirrel ventured close to her. The whole woodlands were full of happiness today.

'Oh dear,' she sighed at last when her song was finished. 'Why do they still treat me like a child?'

'Who?' hooted the owl.

'Aunt Flora and Fauna and Merryweather,' Briar Rose replied.

She walked on still further until at last she came to a woodland pool. The sunlight sparkled on the clear cool water. It looked so inviting on such a hot day that she sat down, and began dabbling her feet in the edge.

'They never want me to meet anyone,' she went on as still more birds and animals gathered around her. 'But you know something? I fooled them. I have met someone!'

'Who?' hooted the owl again, 'Who? Who?'

'Oh, a Prince,' Briar Rose smiled. She looked up at a row of birds on a branch above her. 'Well, he's tall and handsome, and so romantic,' she went on, a dreamy expression on her face. 'Oh, we walk together and talk together, and just before we say goodbye he takes me in his arms . . . and then I wake up!'

The squirrel and the chipmunk shook their heads knowingly.

'Yes, it's only in my dreams,' Briar Rose sighed. 'But they say if you dream a thing more than once, it's sure to come true, and I've seen him so many times.'

The squirrel had noticed something hanging up in a tree not very far away. It was a cloak and hat, made from the finest materials, but dripping wet. He rubbed his eyes to make sure that he wasn't dreaming, throwing aside the acorn which he had been nibbling. It bounced on the owl's head.

'Who, who, who, who, who!' the owl hooted, and the rest of the birds and creatures looked up. The squirrel beckoned for them to follow him.

A few minutes later he proudly showed them the hat and cloak which he had spotted. Mischievously, the squirrel reached for the hat, and in attempting to try it on, covered himself completely.

Down below them the Prince was talking to his horse.

'You know, Samson,' he was saying, 'there was something strange about that voice. It was too beautiful to be real. Maybe it was some mysterious being. A . . . a wood sprite, or a . . .'

The rabbits had located the Prince's boots lying behind him. Slowly, an inch at a time, they began to drag them back into the surrounding undergrowth. The Prince caught a faint sound, and whirling round he saw the rabbits hopping off in his boots.

'Here! Stop!' he yelled.

Up above, the bluebird and cardinal were wrapping the cloak around the owl. The squirrel put the hat on the owl's head, the owl lost his footing, and tumbled down, landing on top of the rabbits and they all rolled over in a heap.

Briar Rose sat up, realising that some mischief was afoot amongst her animal friends. As she parted the undergrowth, her eyes widened. Surely, now she *must* be dreaming.

'Why, it's my Dream Prince!' she gasped, and then added, 'Your Highness!'

'You know,' Briar Rose said as she walked into the clearing, 'I'm not supposed to speak to strangers, but we've met before.'

Leaning against the trunk of a tree she started to sing:

I know you,
I walked with you once upon a dream.
I know you,
The gleam in your eyes is so familiar a gleam.
Yet I know it's true that visions are seldom all
they seem,
But if I know you,
I know what you'll do,
You'll love me at once,
The way you did once upon a dream.

Taking the prince's clothes from the owl, and the boots from the rabbits, she put them on and began to dance, all the birds and beasts joining in. The handsome prince smiled as he watched.

'Who, who, who, who, who' hooted the owl.

Suddenly, Briar Rose felt frightened and, as she turned to run away, the Prince caught her by the hand and held her.

'Oh,' Briar Rose gasped, blushing.

'I'm awfully sorry,' the Prince said, looking embarrassed too. 'I didn't mean to frighten you.'

'Oh . . . it . . . wasn't that,' Briar Rose stammered. 'It's just that you're a . . . a . . .'

'A stranger?' The Prince looked crestfallen. 'But don't you remember, we've met before?' he added.

'We . . . we have?' Briar Rose had a look of surprise on her face.

'Why, of course. You said so yourself. Once upon a dream . . .'

The Prince fell into step with Briar Rose, and slowly they walked down the leafy path, the birds and animals still following.

I know you,
The gleam in your eyes . . .

The Prince took up the song, his powerful young voice ringing through the forest. He and Briar Rose danced as they sang. Both knew in their hearts that they were in love. The creatures of the woodlands just watched in astonishment.

'Who are you?' the Prince asked as he finished his song. 'What's your name?'

'Hmm?' Briar Rose had been dreaming of the things she and the Prince would do. 'Oh . . . my name . . . why it's . . . it's . . .'

Suddenly she stopped, and backed away from the Prince, a look of dismay on her beautiful face. 'Oh, no, no, I can't . . . I . . .' she ducked under a branch, ran a little way, and then turned back to look at her Prince. 'Goodbye.'

'But . . . when will I see you again?' The Prince looked so sad and downcast.

'Oh, never! Never!' sobbed Briar Rose.

'Never?'

'Well . . .' Briar Rose was sorry to see the woebegone expression on the prince's face. 'Maybe some day.'

'When? Tomorrow?' The Prince wished that he could call Briar Rose back, and persuade her to stay forever.

'Oh, no, this evening!' she hastened to add, knowing in her heart that she could not say goodbye to her Prince.

'At the cottage in the clearing,' she called, turning to run.

The Prince untethered his horse, and started to follow in the direction which she had taken.

CHAPTER FIVE

Fauna lit the candles on top of the cake which she had made. As she did so, it started to topple, and she was just in time to catch it, and support it with the handle of a broom.

'There!' she cried, standing back. She glanced at Flora and Merryweather who were just finishing off the dress. 'What do you think of it?'

'Why, it's a very unusual cake, isn't it?' Flora smiled, trying very hard not to laugh as candles and icing slid off the top of the cake.

'Yes, of course it will be much better after it's baked,' Fauna remarked without much confidence, and then cast her eye on the dress.

'It . . . it's not exactly the way it is in the book, is it?' she remarked, shaking her head.

Flora looked rather hurt.

'Oh, I thought I'd improved on it,' she replied. 'But perhaps if I added a few more ruffles, ah, uh, what do you think?'

'Uh huh . . . ah . . . I think so,' said Fauna, looking at Merryweather. 'What do you think, Merryweather?'

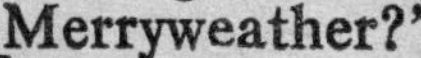

'I think we've had enough of this nonsense,' said Merryweather curtly, shaking herself.

The dress fell to pieces and dropped to the floor. 'I think we ought to think of Briar Rose, and what she'll think of this mess.' She hopped down from the stool on which she had been standing, and headed towards the stairs. 'I still think what I thunk before. *I'm going to get those wands!*'

'You know, I think she's right,' Fauna sighed as Merryweather mounted the stairs.

A few minutes later Merryweather came back downstairs carrying three shining wands.

'Here they are,' she said, handing one each to the other two. 'Good as new.'

'Uh . . . uh . . . uh,' Flora was ill at ease, glancing all around her. 'Careful, Merryweather. Quick! Lock the doors. Fauna, you close the windows. Plug up every cranny. We can't take any chances.'

Quickly they carried out Flora's bidding. Only when all the entrances had been secured did Flora breathe a sigh of relief.

'Now,' she urged. 'You take care of the cake, Fauna, whilst Merryweather cleans up the room, and I'll make the dress. Now hurry!'

Merryweather waved her wand.

Oh, c'mon bucket, mop, broom,
Flora says clean up the room.

The bucket, mop, and broom suddenly came to life and began to clean the room. Flora waved her wand.

And now to make a lovely dress,
Fit to grace a fair Princess.

The fallen pieces of material suddenly began piecing themselves together. Fauna pointed her wand at the cooking ingredients.

'Eggs, flour, milk. Just do it like it says here in the book. I'll put on the candles.'

Flour, eggs and milk poured themselves into the mixing bowl, and the spoon began to beat, stir and batter them.

Flora looked up as the dress changed from pink to blue. A wave of her wand and it changed back to pink. All the time the Three Good Fairies had to keep on dodging the mop and broom as they went about their tasks.

Merryweather waved her wand at the dress.

'Make it blue,' she snapped.

Slowly the dress began to change back from pink to blue.

'Uh! Pink!' Flora waved her wand angrily.

'Blue!' yelled Merryweather.

Flora stepped in front of the dress, and her own clothing turned blue. Merryweather, doubled up with mirth, found her own garments turning to blue. A battle ensued between the two fairies as they began throwing pink and blue magic at each other, and then it was ricocheting all round the room, even spouting out of the chimney.

The raven as it flew over the forest spotted the pink and blue magic shooting out of the chimney. He glided lower to investigate, and settled on the roof.

Inside the cottage Flora and Merryweather were still throwing magic at each other. The dress lying on the table got hit by pink and blue magic, and turned multi-coloured. In dismay Flora and Merryweather gazed at it.

'Oh, now look what you've done!' Flora cried.

'Shhh!' Fauna turned to them. 'Listen!'

'It's Briar Rose!' Merryweather looked round in alarm.

'She's back!' Flora snapped. 'Enough of this foolishness!'

Quickly Flora turned the dress back to pink. Fauna lit the candles on the cake.

'Now, hide on the stairs,' Flora whispered.

As the Three Good Fairies made for the stairs, Merryweather glanced back at the dress.

'Make it blue!' she whispered.

The dress turned back to blue. Then the three of them were hid on the stairs.

'Aunt Flora!' Breathlessly, her cheeks flushed with excitement, Briar Rose ran down the garden path. Flora, Fauna and Merryweather kept silent. They wanted to see her expression when she noticed the dress and the cake.

'Good gracious!' Flora suddenly gave an alarmed whispered exclamation. 'Who left the mop running?'

'Stop, Mop!' commanded Merryweather, and the mop, hit by the magic, fell to the floor.

Briar Rose burst into the cottage.

'Aunt Flora, Fauna, Merryweather . . .' she stopped when she saw that they weren't in sight. 'Where is everybody?'

Then she noticed the cake, and the dress draped over a chair.

'Oh!' she exclaimed, unable to believe what she saw.

'Surprise! Surprise! Surprise!' The Three Good Fairies stood up on the stairs. Briar Rose ran towards them.

'Oh, you darlings! This is the happiest day of my life. Why, everything's so wonderful. Just wait till you meet him.'

'Him?' There was an alarmed expression on Fauna's face.

'Rose!' Merryweather cried in shocked amazement.

'You . . . you've met some stranger?' Flora's voice trembled.

'Oh, he's not a stranger,' Briar Rose laughed. 'We've met before.'

'You have?' Flora gasped.

'Where?' demanded Merryweather.

Briar Rose stepped back, and closing her eyes, she started to sing, 'I walked with you once upon a dream.'

'She's in love,' Fauna whispered.

'Oh, no!' Merryweather clasped her hands to her head.

'This is terrible!' Flora moaned.

'Why?' Briar Rose could not understand why the three of them were so distressed at her news. 'After all, I am sixteen,' she added.

'It isn't that, dear,' Flora took hold of Briar Rose's hands, a pained expression on her face. 'You see . . . you're already betrothed.'

'Betrothed?' Briar Rose went very pale.

'Since the day you were born,' Merryweather said.

'To Prince Phillip, dear,' Fauna smiled.

'But that's impossible!' Briar Rose threw up her hands in despair. 'How could I marry a Prince? I'd have to be a . . . a . . . a Princess!'

The Three Good Fairies looked at each other.

'But you are a Princess, dear,' Flora

reminded her, feeling deceitful at having hidden this from Briar Rose all those sixteen years. 'You're Princess Aurora. Tonight we're taking you back to your father, King Stefan!'

Up on the chimney the raven jumped up and down in excitement. He could hardly believe his luck.

'But . . . but . . . I can't,' Briar Rose exclaimed. 'He's coming here tonight. I promised to meet him!'

'I'm sorry, child!' Flora looked very stern. 'But you must never see that young man again!'

'Oh, no, no!' Briar Rose recoiled. 'I can't believe it. No. No!'

Suddenly, Briar Rose ran up the stairs in a flood of tears.

The Three Good Fairies looked at each other. They, too, were very unhappy now.

'And we thought she'd be so happy.' Flora started to cry also.

CHAPTER SIX

King Stefan looked out of the window of his castle anxiously scanning the countryside which lay before him. Behind him at a table sat King Hubert, who was greedily stuffing himself with food.

'No sign of her yet, Hubert,' King Stefan muttered impatiently, anxiety in his heart.

'Of course not,' King Hubert laughed, clasping his hands together. 'There's a good half hour until sunset yet. Ah, now, come on, man, buck up. Battle's over. The girl's as good as here.'

'I'm sorry, Hubert,' King Stefan smiled. 'But after sixteen years of worrying, never knowing . . .'

'The past, all in the past.' He turned as a servant entered carrying a tray with wine and glasses on it. 'Tonight we toast the future with something I've been saving for sixteen years. Ha ha! Here's to the future!'

'Right Hubert.' King Stefan cast his fears aside as their glasses touched. 'To the future!'

Together they began to sing:

SLEEPING BEAUTY
A toast to this night,
The outlook is rosy,
The future is bright,
Our children will marry,
Our Kingdoms unite.

'Ahem!' King Hubert pretended not to notice that the servant had also sneaked a drink for himself. 'An excellent vintage!'

King Hubert poured each of them another drink.

'To the new home!' he toasted.

'New home?' King Stefan looked surprised.

'Youngsters need a place of their own,' King Hubert looked very pleased with himself. 'A place to raise their own little brood, eh? Ha, ha.'

'Well, I suppose so . . .' King Stefan hadn't thought that he would be losing Aurora again so soon.

'To the home, then,' they chorused, their glasses clinked, and once more they burst into song:

A toast to the home,
One grander by far than a palace in Rome.

Placing their glasses on the table they began to dance — even the servant joined in. Then after a few minutes they seated themselves at the table.

'Now, to plans,' King Hubert became serious. 'What do you think? Nothing elaborate, of course. Forty bedrooms, dining hall, honeymoon cottage.'

King Hubert held up some plans, and King Stefan gasped in astonishment.

'You mean you're building it already?' he asked.

'Built it, man!' King Hubert slapped the table loudly with the roll of plans. 'Finished! The lovebirds can move in tomorrow!'

'Tomorrow!' King Stefan's jaw dropped. 'But, Hubert, they're not even married yet!'

'We'll take care of that tonight,' King Hubert smiled. 'The wedding will take place the moment they arrive!'

'I haven't even seen my daughter yet,' King Stefan groaned, 'and you're taking her away from me!'

'You're getting my Phillip, aren't you?' King Hubert replied.

'Yes . . . but . . .'

'Want to see our grandchildren, don't we?' King Hubert thrust his face close to the other.

'Of course,' King Stefan admitted.

'Then there's no time to lose,' King Hubert rose to his feet. 'We're both getting on in years. Now . . . for the wedding . . .'

'Be reasonable, Hubert,' King Stefan argued. 'After all, Aurora knows nothing at all of this. It's bound to come as quite a shock!'

'Shock!' King Hubert's face reddened as he started to get angry. 'My Phillip, a shock? What's wrong with my Phillip? Won't your daughter like my son?'

'Now . . .' King Stefan became embarrassed.

'I'm not so sure my son will like your daughter!' King Hubert shouted angrily. 'And, furthermore, I'm not sure my grandchildren will want *you* for a grandfather!'

'Why you unreasonable, pompous, blustering old windbag!' King Stefan lost control of his normally placid temper.

'Unreasonable, pompous! On guard, sir!' King Hubert grabbed up a fish from a plate on the table, wielded it like a sword, and hit

King Stefan on top of the head with a squelching smack.

'I warn you, Hubert,' King Stefan clenched his fists. 'This means war!'

'Forward!' King Hubert advanced on King Stefan swinging the fish above his head. 'For honour! For country! For . . .'

Suddenly they both looked at the fish, and burst out laughing.

'What's all this about, anyway?' King Hubert asked as they sat down again.

'Nothing, Hubert, nothing,' King Stefan murmured.

'The children are bound to fall in love with each other.' King Hubert looked down at his feet, and shuffled them.

'Precisely!' King Stefan breathed a huge sigh of relief now that they were friends again. 'And as for grandchildren, I'll have the royal wood-carvers start work on the cradle tomorrow.'

They raised their glasses again.

'To the Wood-Carvers' Guild,' they murmured.

Then they heard the herald's voice from the courtyard below.

'His Royal Highness, Prince Phillip!'

'Phillip!' King Hubert cried, and with King Stefan at his heels, he dashed down a flight of stone steps and out into the courtyard below.

Phillip dismounted from his horse as the two monarchs rushed to him.

'Phillip! Phillip!' King Hubert embraced him quickly. 'Hurry boy, hurry! Change into something suitable. You can't meet your future bride looking like that!'

Phillip looked down at his dust-stained clothes, mud still clinging to them from his fall into the stream.

'But I *have* already met her, father,' he replied.

'You . . . you have?' King Hubert gasped in astonishment.

'Once upon a dream,' the Prince sighed, remembering his encounter with Briar Rose in the forest.

'Oh, don't be so ridiculous!' King Hubert snorted, grasping his son and holding tightly on to him.

'Put me down!' Phillip snapped.

'Now, what's all this dream nonsense?' King Hubert snapped.

'It wasn't only a dream, father,' Phillip protested. 'I really did meet her.'

'Good heavens!' King Hubert cried. 'The Princess Aurora? Goodness me! We must tell Stefan. Why this is the most . . .'

'I . . . I didn't say it was Aurora,' Phillip replied.

'You most certainly did,' King Hubert contradicted him. 'You said that . . .'

'I said I met the girl I was going to marry.' Phillip tried to push him away. 'I have no idea who she was. A peasant girl, I suppose.'

'A . . . a peasant girl?' King Hubert stammered. 'A . . . you're going to marry a . . . a . . . Phillip, you're joking, aren't you? You can't do this to me. Give up the throne of the Kingdom for some . . . some . . . nobody! I won't have it! You're a Prince, and you're going to marry a Princess!'

'Now Father,' Phillip rested a hand on his

shoulder. 'You're living in the past. This is the fourteenth century. Nowadays . . .'

'Nowadays I'm still the King, and I command you to come to your senses . . .'

'And marry the girl I love,' Phillip added. 'Goodbye, Father!'

With that he swung back up into the saddle, and began to ride back towards the castle gates.

'Come back, Phillip!' his father shouted, but he realised it was futile. 'How ever will I be able to tell Stefan?'

CHAPTER SEVEN

The Three Good Fairies and Briar Rose walked sadly through the forest. They spoke little for they all knew that this was the day when they would part company for ever.

At last the castle came into sight, and as they crossed the drawbridge which led into the courtyard their hearts were heavy.

They passed through the courtyard, climbed up a narrow winding staircase and eventually came to a long narrow hallway. Flora was in the lead as they stepped through a narrow doorway which led into a smaller room.

'Bolt the door, Merryweather,' she commanded. 'Pull the curtains, Fauna. And now, Briar Rose, if you'll just sit here . . .'

As Briar Rose seated herself on a chair, Flora advanced towards her.

'This one last gift, dear child, for thee,' she smiled, 'the symbol of royalty. A crown to wear in grace and beauty, as is they right and royal duty.'

As Briar Rose caught a glimpse of herself in the mirror, she began to cry.

'Now dear,' said Flora, slipping a comforting arm around her, 'I think you'd appreciate a few moments alone.'

With that the Three Good Fairies withdrew, closing the door behind them. They huddled into an alcove in the main hall.

'It's that boy she met,' Merryweather sighed.

'Whatever are we going to do?' Fauna asked.

Briar Rose was left alone sobbing. Slowly the fire in the fireplace burnt down until only the smouldering embers were left. Then, suddenly, smoke began to rise, taking on a definite shape as it billowed out into the room. *Maleficent*! The Witch had arrived!

Outside in their alcove the Three Good Fairies were deep in conference.

'I don't see why she has to marry any old Prince,' Merryweather muttered.

'That's not for us to decide, dear,' Fauna sighed. 'Maybe we should tell King Stefan about the boy.'

'Well, why don't we?' Merryweather asked.

Then, the three of them heard voices from within the room where Briar Rose sat sobbing.

'Maleficent!' gasped Flora.

They rushed into the room. It had become dark, and at first they were unable to see anything.

'Rose! Rose!' Flora shouted.

They caught a glimpse of Briar Rose disappearing into the fireplace in a cloud of smoke.

'Oh, why ever did we leave her alone?' they wailed.

The Three Good Fairies advanced on the fireplace. Flora waved her wand. The fireplace disappeared at once, and they hurried through the wall.

'Rose, Rose. Where are you?' they shouted frantically. 'Where are you?'

Beyond the fireplace was a narrow winding staircase up which Briar Rose had gone at the command of the wisp of smoke which was really Maleficent in one of her disguises.

The fairies hurried in her wake, yelling for her to stop, but it was to no avail. She was now in Maleficent's power! They searched frantically in every room which they passed, but there was no sign of her.

Meanwhile, Briar Rose had followed the wisp of smoke into an upper room. She stood hypnotised as it wafted up and down in the centre, finally transforming itself into — a spinning-wheel! In a trance she advanced upon it, reaching out, her fingers grasping for the spindle.

'Rose! Rose!' the Three Good Fairies cried, bursting into the room, horrified at what they saw. 'Rose! Don't touch anything!'

Briar Rose snatched her hand away at their warning.

'Touch the spindle!' Maleficent's voice filled the room. 'Touch it, I say!'

A struggle was going on inside Briar Rose. Her hand hovered over the spindle, and then before she realised it the needle had pricked her finger.

'You poor simple fools!' Maleficent transformed into her own shape out of the smoke, grinning evilly in triumph. 'Thinking you could defeat me. *Me!* The Mistress of all Evil!'

The Three Good Fairies looked on in horror. Briar Rose slowly sank to the floor, lying still and pale. They knew that they had failed!

'Well,' Maleficent backed away, 'here's your precious Princess!'

Suddenly there was a burst of flames and a cloud of smoke, and Maleficent was gone.

'Oh, I'll never forgive myself,' Flora sobbed.

'We're all to blame,' Fauna tried to console her.

They sank to their knees beside Briar Rose.

King Stefan and his Queen sat on the throne in the crowded room. King Hubert entered, a worried look on his face.

'Stefan,' he whispered in the King's ear. 'There's . . . there's something important I . . . I have to tell you.'

'Not now, Hubert,' said King Stefan impatiently.

'But . . . it's about Phillip,' King Hubert had a distinct note of urgency in his voice.

'Phillip?' King Stefan looked surprised. 'Why, where is the boy? Send for him immediately. He should be here by now!'

'But . . .'

'Shhh!' King Stefan motioned him to be silent as the herald began to speak.

'The sun has set,' the herald announced in a loud voice. 'Make ready to welcome your Princess!'

In the room upstairs the Three Good Fairies realised that they had no hope of reviving Aurora. They managed to carry her to a bed where they placed covers over her, and all the while tears rolled down their cheeks.

They went out on to the balcony in despair. Below them in the courtyard fireworks were being let off, and crowds of people were cheering in anticipation of a royal wedding.

'Poor King Stefan and the Queen,' Flora sobbed. 'They'll be heartbroken when they find out!'

Flora looked at the other two, and began wiping away her tears.

'They're not going to,' she said.

'But . . .' Fauna began.

'We'll put them all to sleep,' Flora replied, 'and they will stay that way until Briar Rose awakens!'

Flora waved her wand and the three of them became tiny once again. Then, flying down from the balcony, they began to spread sleep-dust over the waiting crowds. A soldier on

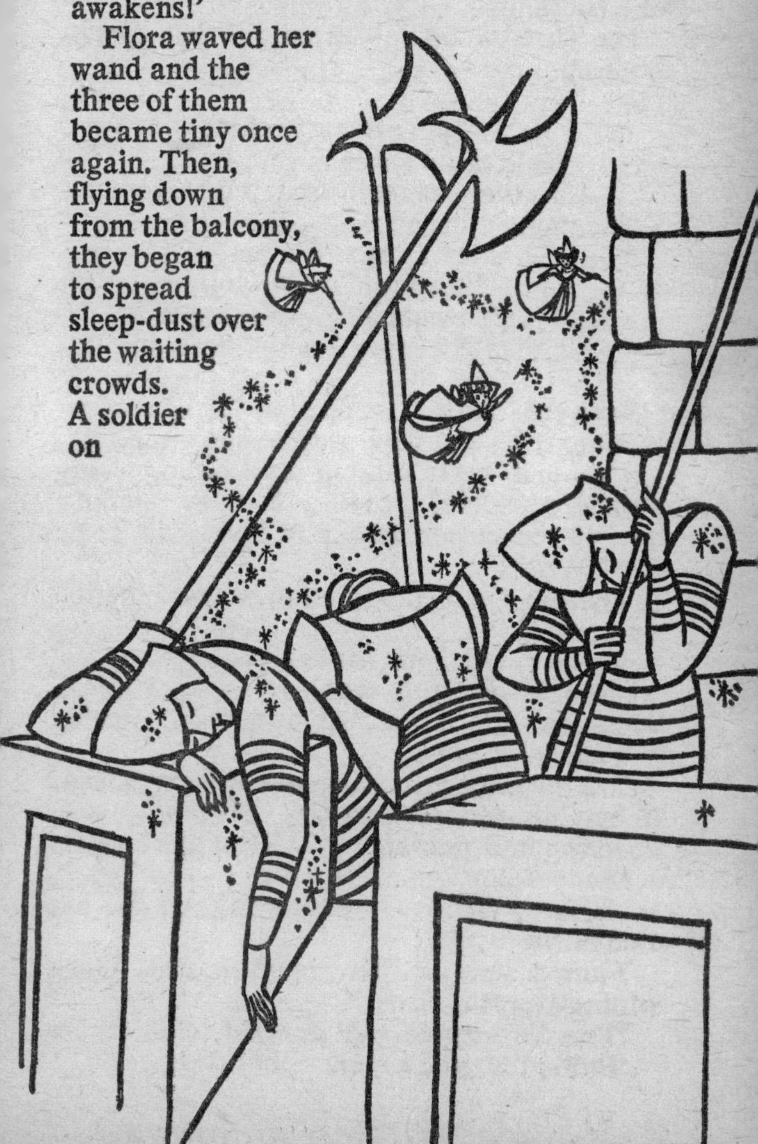

guard by the gate was the first to yawn, and slumped to the ground. Soon everybody was following suit.

The Three Good Fairies sang as they spread the sleep-dust:

Sleeping Beauty fair,
Gold of sunshine in your hair,
Lips that shame the red, red rose,
Dreaming of true love in slumber repose,
One day he will come,
Riding out of the dawn,
And you'll awaken to love's first kiss,
'Till then, Sleeping Beauty, sleep on.

Even the fountain stopped as the sleep-dust fell onto it. Everywhere people were sleeping.

'I've just been talking to Phillip,' King Hubert whispered drowsily in King Stefan's ear. 'It seems he's fallen in love with some peasant girl . . .'

'Peasant girl?' King Stefan yawned loudly. 'Yes, yes . . .'

His eyes closed and his head nodded.

Flora hovered in front of King Hubert. Reaching out, she pulled at his moustache, and his eyes opened.

'The peasant girl. Who is she?' she asked. 'Where did he meet her?'

'Just some peasant girl,' Hubert's eyelids began to droop again.

'Where? Where?' Flora tugged on his moustache again.

'Oh . . . huh . . .' Hubert mumbled. 'Once upon a dream . . .'

Flora flew up to a huge chandelier where Merryweather and Fauna were sitting.

'Come on!' she cried. 'We've got to get back to the cottage!'

'Why? Why?' they looked amazed.

'Come on!' Flora urged. 'We've no time to lose!'

Night had fallen by the time the prince reached the cottage in the clearing. Dismounting, he walked up to the door, and knocked lightly.

'Come in,' a voice called.

He pushed open the door, and stepped inside. It was dark, and he hesitated, unable to see who it was who sat in front of the dying embers of the fire. All of a sudden, hands seized him, and he was dragged to the ground. He struggled, but there were too many attackers, and within minutes he was a prisoner.

The fire glowed brightly as though somebody had thrown dry tinder upon it and the Prince could see clearly. An evil-looking woman, dressed in black, stood before the fireplace, a raven perched on her shoulder.

The horrible little men who held him captive were her servants — *the Goons!* They began binding him with ropes. Maleficent laughed. All her carefully laid plans were now bearing fruit.

'Well,' she cackled. 'This is a pleasant surprise. I set my trap for a peasant, and lo, I catch a Prince!'

She waved a hand at her henchmen.

'Away with him,' she hissed. 'But gently, my pets, gently. I have plans for our royal guest!'

CHAPTER EIGHT

The Three Good Fairies flew as fast as they could back towards the cottage. Once they came in sight of the clearing they paused to change themselves back to full size.

They pushed open the door, and went inside.

'We're too late!' Flora stooped and picked up a hat which lay on the floor. 'Maleficent! She's got Prince Phillip! She's taken him back to the Forbidden Mountain!'

'But we can't,' Fauna gasped. 'We can't go there!'

'We can,' Flora snapped. 'And we must. Come on. There's no time to be lost!'

Maleficent's castle stood in the mountains, shrouded by mist. Dark and forbidding, it was a place to be avoided.

However, the Three Good Fairies knew that somehow or other they had to rescue Prince Phillip. Crouched behind some rocks they looked up at the castle, and their hopes began to fade. There was only one entrance, and that was over a drawbridge where a Goon sentry patrolled.

Without their magical powers the Fairies would never have been able to enter the castle. It did not present much problem to them though. Swiftly they climbed up the drawbridge chains and then fluttered up on to the parapets above, taking advantage of the gargoyles to screen them from prying eyes as they made their way along to a lighted

window. They peeped inside, and saw some Goons dancing around a fire. Beyond the Goons they saw Maleficent sitting on her throne, stroking her pet raven.

'What a pity Prince Phillip can't be here to enjoy the celebration,' she laughed. 'Come! We must go to the dungeon and cheer him up!'

With the raven flying in front of her, Maleficent left the room. The Fairies entered the room by the window, moving slowly, and keeping close to the wall, hoping that the guards would not notice them.

The Goons were too busy dancing. Maleficent was happy, and that made life a lot easier for them. They did not see the Fairies cross the room, and follow Maleficent down to the dungeon.

Keeping some distance behind the Witch, the Fairies saw Maleficent pause before a heavy bolted door. They watched as she entered, the raven perched on her shoulder.

Prince Phillip looked up at Maleficent. He was bound securely with chains, and his expression was one of hopelessness.

'Oh come now, Prince Phillip,' Maleficent sneered. 'Why so melancholy? A wondrous future lies before you, the destined hero of a charming fairy tale come true. Look!'

Maleficent conjured up a vision. Before his eyes Prince Phillip saw King Stefan's castle.

'Behold King Stefan's castle!' Maleficent cried in triumph. 'And in yonder topmost tower, dreaming of her true love . . . the Princess Aurora! But see the gracious whim of fate. Why 'tis the self-same peasant maid who won the heart of our noble prince but yesterday. She is indeed . . .'

The vision changed to one of the slumbering Aurora.

'... most wondrous fair, gold of sunshine in her hair. Lips that shame the red, red rose, in ageless sleep she finds repose. The years roll

by, but a hundred years to a steadfast heart are but a day...'

The vision changed again. This time gates opened and a prince, an old man, rode slowly through into the distance.

'And now the gates of the dungeon open, and our prince is free to go his way. Off he rides on his noble steed, a valiant figure straight and tall, to wake his love with love's first kiss, and prove that true love conquers all.'

Maleficent laughed cruelly at Prince Phillip's expression.

'Why you — you!' Merryweather, beside herself with rage, was about to fly into the cell, but just in time Flora pulled her back.

Maleficent held out her hand, and the raven hopped on to it.

'Come my pet,' she sighed. 'Let us leave our noble prince with these happy thoughts. It has been a most gratifying day.'

Maleficent closed the door, and paused to stroke the raven again, an expression of supreme satisfaction on her evil face.

'For the first time in sixteen years I shall sleep well,' she sighed as she went slowly back up the steps to the tower. Hiding in a crack in the wall, the Three Good Fairies watched her until she was out of sight.

The Fairies entered the cell and then changed themselves back to normal size.

'Shhh!' Flora silenced the Prince's questions with a wave of her hand. 'No time to explain.'

Using her magic wand she burned the shackles off his hands and feet. Merryweather set to work to burn the lock off the door.

Prince Phillip stood up, and strode towards the open door, but Flora caught at his sleeve and pulled him back.

'Wait, Prince Phillip!' she cried. 'The road to true love may be barred by still many more dangers, which you alone will have to face.'

She waved her wand, and before the startled Prince could reply, a shining sword and shield appeared in his hand.

'So arm thyself with this enchanted Shield of Virtue', Flora went on, 'and this mighty Sword of Truth, for these weapons of righteousness will triumph over evil. Now come, we must hurry!'

The Prince followed the Three Good Fairies as they stepped out into the passage. There was a sudden movement above them, a flap of wings, and then with a squawk Maleficent's raven flew off ahead of them.

The bird croaked out a loud warning, and then they heard the running footsteps of the approaching Goons. As the guards appeared round the corner, the Fairies saw that the raven was in the lead.

With another wave of their wands, the Three Good Fairies made themselves tiny again. The Prince took up a position on a window-ledge, his sword poised to meet the rushing Goons.

The Goons were forced back by the slashing magic blade, and then the Fairies and Prince Phillip jumped out of the window and ran along a ledge. From there it was only a short jump to the courtyard below where a horse stood tethered.

The Fairies hovered around Phillip as he untied the horse. Goons had appeared amongst some boulders above them.

'Phillip! Watch out!' Flora shouted her warning as the first boulders began to move, toppling down towards the Prince. Then she remembered her magic. Sixteen years living as a mortal in the cottage in the woods had almost made her forget her powers. Her wand came up. Just as the boulders were about to crush Phillip they were suddenly transformed into bubbles, floating on down into the courtyard, and bursting against the walls.

The Goons began firing arrows. The Fairies quickly darted behind Phillip's shield where they knew they were safe. Again they used their magic. Arrows of death turned into harmless flowers, floating gently earthwards.

By this time the Prince was mounted, and with the Three Good Fairies flying behind, they headed towards the drawbridge. Some Goons tried to prevent their escape by pouring boiling oil from the parapets, but Flora's magic turned it into a rainbow.

A speck appeared in the sky behind them. It was the raven, as evil as his mistress. Merryweather broke off from the others, and flew up to intercept him. The bird, fearing more magic, turned back in the direction of the castle, eventually settling on a balcony. With a wave of her wand, Merryweather turned the raven to stone!

Maleficent came out on to the balcony. She had heard the shouting of the Goons and wondered what was going on. She noticed the raven out of the corner of her eye.

'Silence!' she snarled. 'You tell those fools to . . . no! Oh, no!'

She saw only too well that the raven had been turned to stone. A terrible rage filled her, and with evil in her heart she began climbing the steps to the top of the tower. She would stop them escaping at all costs!

The drawbridge was being raised by more Goons. The Fairies flew beneath it, shooting magic at it with their wands. Just in time the galloping Prince rode on to it, and his horse cleared the gap, landing on a cliff beyond.

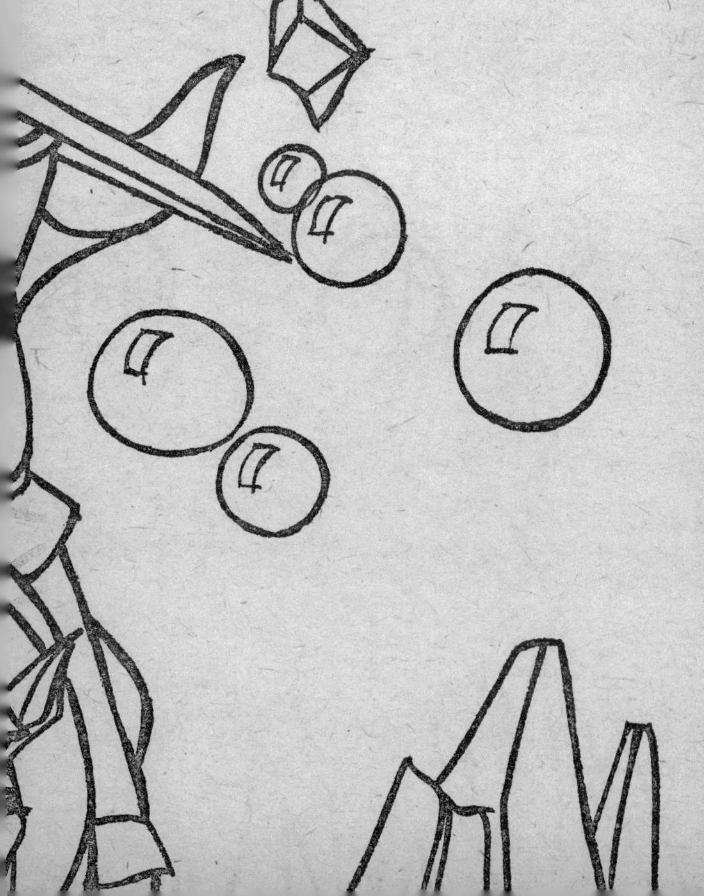

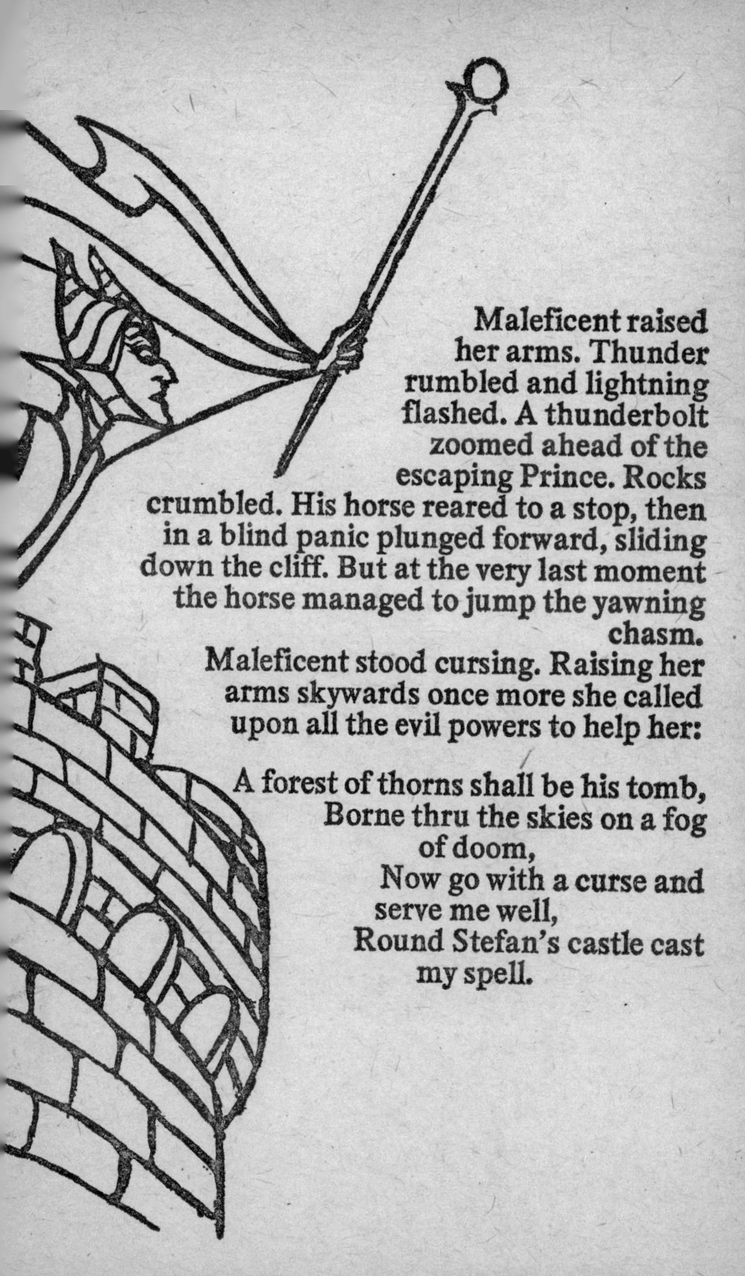

Maleficent raised her arms. Thunder rumbled and lightning flashed. A thunderbolt zoomed ahead of the escaping Prince. Rocks crumbled. His horse reared to a stop, then in a blind panic plunged forward, sliding down the cliff. But at the very last moment the horse managed to jump the yawning chasm.

Maleficent stood cursing. Raising her arms skywards once more she called upon all the evil powers to help her:

A forest of thorns shall be his tomb,
Borne thru the skies on a fog of doom,
Now go with a curse and serve me well,
Round Stefan's castle cast my spell.

CHAPTER NINE

Prince Phillip, with the Fairies flying above him, pulled up sharply as he came into sight of King Stefan's castle. He could barely see the place for a thick forest of thorns had grown up around it, and a thorn hedge barricaded the road ahead of him.

It seemed as though he had been beaten after all, but undaunted he drew his sword. It seemed to vibrate with power in his hand. He was surprised at the ease with which he could cut through the jungle of thorns. The Three Good Fairies flew above his head, watching his progress with bated breath. Somehow they sensed that Maleficent was not beaten yet.

Maleficent in fact had been overlooking them from her castle with her supernatural powers of sight. She cursed as she saw that her barrier of thorns had not halted Prince Phillip.

'No!' she snarled. 'It cannot be!'

In a whirlwind of magic she took off, flying through the air, and heading towards King Stefan's castle.

'Now you shall deal with me, oh Prince,' she fumed, 'and all the Powers of Hell!'

Prince Phillip looked up in amazement as sparks landed on his shield. His horse shied in fear, and the Three Good Fairies drew back in fright.

A dragon barred their way, a huge monster with green scales and flames hissing from its slavering jaws, roaring in anger.

The Prince controlled his horse, murmuring words of encouragement to it as he did so. Then, his sword in one hand and his shield in the other, he charged forward.

Flame stabbed from the dragon's mouth. The horse reared, and Phillip felt

himself sailing through the air to land with a bump on the ground. The horse bolted, and the fearsome monster towered up over the Prince.

He dodged the first burst of flame, the very heat of it leaving a crater in the ground. The dragon wheeled round. Then came a second blast of fire. Prince Phillip threw up his shield to protect himself, and staggered back. Then he ran back into the thorn forest.

The dragon moved in to search for him, and a game of hide and seek began, with death as the loser's lot. Hiding behind a thorn bush the prince watched as the dragon's head came into view. He then struck with his sword. The wounded beast roared in pain and anger, and breathed fire again, some of the flames licking at the dry thorns and igniting them.

Within minutes there was a blazing forest fire. Phillip found himself cut off and cornered at the base of a cliff, the fire creeping closer all the time. The heat was intolerable, scorching his skin. It seemed that Maleficent had won after all!

Suddenly, he saw Flora hovering above him.

'Up this way,' she called.

With her help he struggled up the cliff and was almost at the top when he saw the dragon coming up after him! Flames could not harm this fearsome beast, and now it was bent on revenge. It was also able to climb much quicker than him, and just as he gained the top of the cliff he could feel the terrible heat from its fire licking at his boots.

With the fairies watching anxiously, Phillip backed away from the beast. Behind him was

a long drop down to the blazing inferno below. Before him was the advancing dragon!

At the first blast his shield was knocked into the abyss of flames beneath. Clutching his sword, Phillip resigned himself to a valiant death; but there was no thought of surrender in his mind. He would die fighting to the last.

Suddenly Flora hovered above him, sprinkling some dust on to his sword.

'Now Sword of Truth fly swift and sure, that evil die and good endure!' she chanted.

Phillip looked up. He knew what he had to do. Changing his stance, he gripped the sword like a spear, and flung it at the dragon with all his might, praying that his aim would be true.

The sword sped straight to the head of the dragon, burying itself in the scaly head up to the hilt. With a roar of rage the beast made one last desperate lunge which Phillip nimbly dodged, and then it was gone forever over the steep cliff. Phillip peered down, but all he could see was flames everywhere.

For a brief second the smoke cleared, and he was afforded one glimpse of his sword lying far below, impaled in Maleficent's cloak. She would trouble him no more!

The dark clouds and the thorns had disappeared. The way to the castle was clear.

Prince Phillip walked across the courtyard, the fairies flying above him. All around them people slumbered peacefully, and would continue to do so forever unless . . .

Phillip followed the Three Good Fairies up the long flight of stone steps, and into the room where Aurora lay on a bed, her eyes closed, scarcely breathing.

He dropped to his knees at her side. She was the same beautiful maid whom he had met in the woods. She was his Princess, too. All he had to do was to awaken her . . .

His lips brushed hers in a gentle kiss. At first it seemed as though nothing had happened, and then one eyelid flickered open. Both eyes opened, and she smiled weakly as she sat up.

Below them in the courtyard the people were waking up, too. The fountain started to flow again. Soldiers yawned, stretched and picked up their fallen weapons.

In the throne-room King Stefan shook himself.

'Ah, uh . . . oh . . .' he grunted. 'Forgive me, Hubert, the wine. Now, ah, you, ah, were saying . . .'

'Oh . . . oh . . . yes.' King Hubert struggled to sit up. 'Oh yes, well, after all, Stefan, this *is* the fourteenth century. Well, to come to the point, my son Phillip says he's going to marry a . . .'

A blast of trumpets drowned his words. Then down the stairway, arm in arm, came Phillip and Aurora. People cheered, and more trumpets blew.

'It's Aurora!' King Stefan gasped. 'She's here!'

'And . . . and . . . and,' King Hubert was beside himself with joy and excitement, 'and Phillip!'

Aurora ran to the Queen, and hugged her. Tears ran down both their faces. King Stefan gently stroked his daughter's hair.

'What . . . what . . . does this mean, boy?' King Hubert stammered. 'I . . . I don't understand.'

Up above on the balcony Flora, Fauna and Merryweather looked at each other. Tears were streaming down their faces, too.

'Why, Fauna, what's the matter dear?' Flora sobbed.

'Oh, I just love happy endings,' Fauna wept.

'Yes, I do, too,' Flora replied. 'Blue?'

They peered down to determine the final colour of Aurora's dress. It was blue.

'Pink!' Flora commanded, and waved her wand.

'Blue!' Merryweather changed it immediately.

Amongst the crowded dancers the colour of the Princess's dress kept changing from blue to pink, but nobody seemed to notice.

Everybody was singing happily:

I know you,
I walked with you once upon a dream
I know you,
The gleam in your eyes is so familiar a gleam;
Yet I know it's true that visions are seldom
all they seem,
But if I know you,
I know what you'll do,
You'll love me at once,
The way you did once upon a dream.

The Three Good Fairies prepared to leave. None of the people were aware that they had been in a long deep sleep. But everybody was happy, and that was all that mattered. Everything had turned out happily at last.

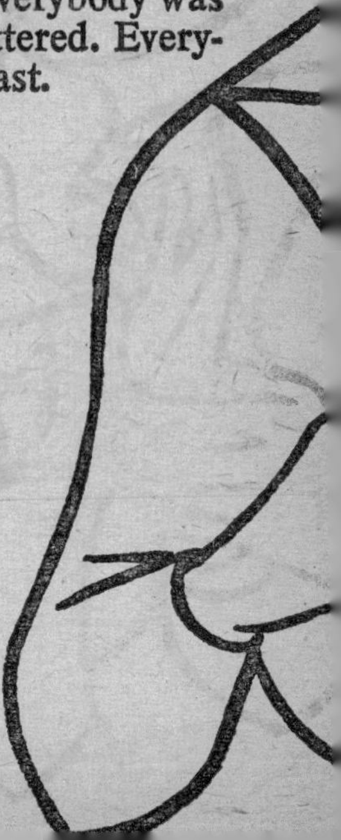

© WALT DISNEY PRODUCTIONS

One of the most
beautiful books ever
published~now
available as a large,
low priced quality
paperback